THE WAY OF HEAVEN

CONTENTS

INTRODUCTION

What is the most important human activity? This book is my answer to that question.

It describes a practice as old as humanity itself, a way of life followed by the truly wise of all ages. I call it the Way of Heaven. It's the path of those who daily seek God, hear Him, and follow His guidance.

Heaven has a way of doing things. Contrary to what some mistakenly believe, far from being a passive observer, Heaven is an active provider of information, wisdom, and direction.

Heavenly data is always wholly accurate, and utterly relevant to our earthly situation. Because of its uniqueness in this respect, the guidance of Heaven is to be sought before that of all other sources.

Earth can show us many things, but I am convinced that only Heaven can consistently reveal exactly what we need to know at any given moment, in order to live life most fully. To live by this inspiration is to take the Way of Heaven. There is, in my view, no higher path than this.

We are given one mortal life on earth, and during our relatively brief time here, we can either do things our way, or Heaven's way. A life lived without Heaven's guidance is a life lived in the dark, but a life of contemplation is always bright, shining forever.

The Way of Heaven is open to all. Those who take it join an invisible company of men and women from every continent and century who have diligently sought and followed the Way.

Simon Gibson

I
INSPIRATION

Inspiration is no rarity. It is to the soul what breath is to the body. The word may be used to describe both the process of breathing in, and the process by which the soul is energised. Just as the taking of physical breath is an involuntary act, so is the breathing of the soul.

Everyone is inspired by something. Each experiences being stirred by emotion, or being gripped by the urge to do something. Each experiences sudden ideas or insights. Each experiences the desire, the confidence, or the enthusiasm to do certain things. Whether by joy or woe, by mirth or melancholy, we are all inspired.

But just as the air we breathe may be fresh or stale, pure or polluted, dry or damp, that which inspires the soul varies in its character, quality, and consequences. The capacity for inspiration doesn't guarantee that what inspires will be good for us. Inspiration may be constructive or destructive, functional or dysfunctional, pro-social or anti-social.

Inspired by noble principles we may achieve a great deal of good, adding meaning and value to our own lives as well as to the lives of others. History contains a great many stories of those who have made such a difference, though many of these are unwritten, unsung, or even unrecognised. In contrast stands the influence of those whose inspirations flow from less noble sources. That's all of us, at one time or another.

When inspiration is unhelpful, the scale of its impact can range from the ineffective to the deadly. Thankfully, the effects of bad inspiration may die unborn, as when such emotions, ideas, and urges, are dismissed, rather than entertained and acted upon. But where the seeds of the unhelpful and ignoble find friendly soil in which to take root, it is a different story. Their fruit invariably betrays their origins and nature, through consequences that sooner or later prove damaging both to the individual and to others unfortunate enough to be within the range of influence.

Such consequences can be as destructive as death itself. I'm not just talking about those who set out consciously and deliberately to take life, but the much larger group of those whose inspiration, although not intended by them to yield this outcome, results nevertheless in fatal consequences. The person driven by an anger that has never been properly controlled, the one obsessed by compulsive dieting yet never satisfied with their body image, and the driver who speeds confidently whilst under the influence of drugs or alcohol, are all examples of those whose inspiration may kill.

I am reminded of a Russian short story that was set in Hell. Two men were in adjacent cauldrons, but they were being treated so differently that one complained to the supervising demon, saying, "Why is it that I am being boiled so vigorously, whilst my neighbour appears to be receiving little more than a warm bath? All I did was to write a few novels, but he is a murderer!" The demon replied, "Yes, it is true that you were a writer and that he was a murderer, but whilst he murdered one man in a moment of uncontrolled anger, your books have negatively influenced the lives of thousands, resulting in a great many injuries, thefts, rapes, and murders. That is why you are now receiving the greater punishment."

How can we ensure that the inspiration we receive and follow is always good, and that we never yield to the bad? The answer is that by ourselves we cannot. Whilst it is absolutely right that we make every effort to achieve this goal, we face two major existential limitations.

Firstly, however intelligent and qualified we may be, we remain limited in knowledge and wisdom. This means that even in circumstances where we believe that we are doing the right thing, it is possible that, were we to be in possession of all the data relating to the situation, we would realise that there was a better course of action, and proceed differently. Limited knowledge guarantees limited goodness. Only by communicating with an all-knowing and all-wise source, may we escape from this limitation.

Secondly, however strong and determined we may be, we remain limited in power. This means that even when we think we know what is best, we may not be able to achieve it. We may lack the contacts, the resources, the expertise, the time, the opportunity, or we may simply forget. Limited power, like limited knowledge, restricts our ability to do all that we would. Only by connecting with an all-powerful source, may we escape from this limitation.

If we would enjoy the greatest and most constant inspiration, we must transcend the limitations of our finite human nature by becoming friends with a being infinitely more knowledgeable, wise, and powerful than ourselves.

Is such a relationship possible? Moses and Christ both state plainly that it is:

> Man shall not live by bread alone, but by every word that proceeds from the mouth of God.
> Deuteronomy 8:3; Matthew 4:4

Their message is that such a relationship is not only possible, but is a lifestyle open to all, and intended by God for all — the healthiest lifestyle ever known to humanity.

Jesus promises not only a relationship with Infinite Intelligence, but a friendship in which the Spirit of God will lead us *"into all truth" (John 16:13)*, that is, all we need to know in order to live most fully — inside information. He promises a friendship in which we will receive *"power from on high" (Luke 24:49)*, that is, all the power we need in order to do what is good and right. He says:

> You shall receive power when the Holy Spirit has come upon you; and you shall be witnesses to Me in Jerusalem, and in all Judea and Samaria, and to the end of the earth.
> Acts 1:8

Here is inspiration of the highest order – divine inspiration. Many things have the potential to inspire the human heart, but one exceeds all others, just as the generated light of the sun surpasses the reflected light of the moon in brilliance. According to Christ, this is the most important of all human activities, the greatest of all acquisitions, and the sole foundation for the true success of individuals, groups, and nations. He says:

> Blessed are those who hear the word of God and keep it! Luke 11:28

This book is about walking with God, moment by moment, day by day. There can be no greater life than a life spent seeking God, and doing the will of Heaven. By following the ancient principles contained in this book, you can learn how to live in the consciousness of Heaven on earth.

Divine inspiration is the experience of receiving from Heaven. It's both a product and a process, being not only the name we give to what we receive from God, but also the name we use to describe the process by which we receive.

Even as you read these words, God is present with you, invisible yet real. How aware are you of His presence? If I asked you to tell me what God has said to you so far today, would you be able to reply? Whether you have never heard from God, or you occasionally seek Him, or you look to Him daily, my prayer for you is the same: that you will learn to walk with Him as closely as it is possible to do, and that this book will both inspire and assist you in this, the greatest of all endeavours.

But before we proceed further, there is a fundamental question that we must first address.

II
KING OF HEAVEN

Do you believe that there is a God with whom we may have a personal relationship?

The question of God's existence is an important one, for if He does not exist, then the mind that seeks Him is engaged in a futile quest, and the mind that hears Him is engaged in fantasy, or worse, hallucination.

If God exists, loves us, and desires to communicate with us, then to seek Him is not only a sensible activity, but the most important activity that a human may ever undertake. To decline the friendship, guidance, and assistance of the Creator and Sustainer of all, One who loves us purely, fully, and deeply, would be folly indeed.

But does God exist? And if He does, how would we know? The ultimate test must always be that of personal experience. If I am told by others that something is a fact, I may or may not believe it, but if what they say concurs with my personal experience, I will likely agree with them. If, however, it is outside my experience, then I have only their word for it. They may be right, or they may be wrong.

This illustrates two kinds of faith. The first is faith merely at the level of mental assent. This is the case where we hear a proposition and we decide to accept it as true. Consciously or unconsciously, we trust the authority of the proposition's source. The second is faith at the level of spiritual conviction. In this case we have proved to ourselves that a thing is true and we experience an inner knowing or conviction that it is so.

When someone says that they believe in God, they may simply have accepted the proposition that God exists, or they may be describing a conviction born of spiritual experience, and expressed in an ongoing relationship of dependent trust, divine inspiration, and progressive deification. These worlds are as far apart as the galaxies in the heavens.

Belief in the existence of God is not enough. As James says:

> *If a brother or sister be naked, and destitute of daily food, and one of you say to them, "Depart in peace, be warmed and filled," but you do not give them the things which are needed for the body, what does it profit? Thus also faith by itself, if it does not have works, is dead. But someone will say, "You have faith, and I have works." Show me your faith without your works, and I will show you my faith by my works. You believe that there is one God. You do well. Even the demons believe – and tremble! But do you want to know, O foolish man, that faith without works is dead?*
>
> James 2:15-20

To say that the Way of Heaven is the way of those who believe is a correct but potentially misleading description. It is more helpful to describe it as the way of those who know and who follow the King of Heaven.

How do we move from mental assent to walking with God unless we test for ourselves the proposition that God exists, and that He is a good God who loves us? If I have never seen an elephant, but I am told that they exist, I may test this proposition by visiting a zoo that has elephants, or by travelling to a country where elephants are to be found. Should I find an elephant, I will have proven to myself that elephants are real. In the same way, if I wish to test the hypothesis that there is a God who loves me, I must go and see.

Before we make the test, it is important to say something about the nature of the test itself. If I set out to validate the proposition that elephants exist, and I come across an elephant, this single positive sighting proves their existence to me. But what if I find no elephants? Can I assume that my lack of sightings proves that they do not exist? Of course not – I may simply have looked in the wrong place. One positive sighting is proof enough, but my failure to find elephants cannot prove their non-existence. Only if we search all creation in a moment of time, and find no elephants, can we say that there are none. Up to that point we cannot say with certainty that there are no elephants, although a continued lack of sightings may lead us to say that the existence of elephants seems less and less likely. But however unlikely the existence of elephants might seem, without proof either of their existence, or of their non-existence, we cannot be certain, one way or another. Applying this principle to God, we may confidently affirm that the failure of any human to find Him proves nothing whatsoever concerning His existence.

In this book I invite you to test for yourself the proposition that God exists. I do not ask you to take my word for it. Neither do I ask you to take the word of others for it (although there have been a very great number of positive encounters by innumerable people over many centuries). The observations of others may tell us a great deal, but we can only be certain of that which we have proved for ourselves.

Someone may say at this point, "Surely it is in the very nature of faith to not require proof. If there were proof, what need would there be for faith?" Such thinking reflects a profound misunderstanding of the nature of faith in God. According to this commonly held misconception, faith and proof are antithetical. Faith requires no proof, and proof requires no faith.

The truth could not be more different, for faith is born of proof, and proof is the genesis of faith. Think for a moment of your faith in your ability to walk. You are confident that you can, because you have demonstrated your ability in this respect. You have proved to yourself that you can do it. Think of your faith in relation to anyone or anything, and you will find that your level of trust is linked directly to your experience of that person or thing. If you have found someone unreliable, you will trust them less. If you find that each time you buy a particular product it doesn't work properly, you will lose confidence in it, and probably switch to another brand. The lesson from experience is clear: faith and proof are inextricably linked.

There is, of course, such a thing as blind faith, where we choose to believe that a proposition is true, despite the absence of evidence for it, or even in the face of what appears to be evidence to the contrary. Where scripture encourages blind faith it is as a means of coming to God, rather than as a basis for daily relationship with Him.

Notable here is the account of how the disciple Thomas did not believe Christ had been raised from the dead until he had seen Him with his own eyes, physically touched him, and felt his wounds. Initially disbelieving the accounts of the resurrection, it was only when Thomas saw for himself that Jesus was alive, that he believed. Christ's response was to remark on the fact that Thomas had believed on the evidence of his physical senses, and to conclude:

Thomas, because you have seen Me, you have believed. Blessed are those who have not seen and yet have believed. John 20:29

Unfortunately, this passage has been taken by some to indicate that personal experience of God is wholly unnecessary to faith, or even that faith without such experience is somehow more blessed. Such teaching could not be further from the intention of Christ, whose aim, as expressed in His interview with Nicodemus, a Jewish leader, is that men and women might see (i.e. personally experience) the kingdom of God:

> *There was a man of the Pharisees named Nicodemus, a ruler of the Jews. This man came to Jesus by night and said to Him, "Rabbi, we know that You are a teacher come from God; for no one can do these signs that You do unless God is with him." Jesus answered and said to him, "Most assuredly, I say to you, unless one is born again, he cannot see the kingdom of God." Nicodemus said to Him, "How can a man be born when he is old? Can he enter a second time into his mother's womb and be born?" Jesus answered, "Most assuredly, I say to you, unless one is born of water and the Spirit, he cannot enter the kingdom of God. That which is born of the flesh is flesh, and that which is born of the Spirit is spirit. Do not marvel that I said to you, 'You must be born again.' The wind blows where it wishes, and you hear the sound of it, but cannot tell where it comes from and where it goes. So is everyone who is born of the Spirit."* John 3:1-8

Jesus' mission was, and still is, to draw all people to Himself, a relational, and therefore experiential, purpose.

In His response to Thomas, Christ comments on the fact that he believed because he saw, and points out that people do not need to see God physically in order to enter into relationship with Him. We may come to God without any prior experience of Him, just as we may come to a human person that we do not already know, or visit a geographical location to which we have never travelled before. All that is required of us is to make the journey.

However, it is important to note that this is not the same thing as saying that we can have an ongoing personal relationship with God without any experience of Him. Such an idea is ridiculous. It is as crazy as saying that you can build a human friendship without any experience of the other, or that you could enjoy the beauty of a spectacular view without being able to experience it in any way.

Christ's words to Thomas and His words to Nicodemus are complementary. To Thomas He says that physical sight is unnecessary for faith. We may choose to believe, in the absence of any personal proof (mental assent), or we may turn to God, despite not being able to see Him physically, and discover not only that He exists, but that He loves us personally (spiritual conviction). To Nicodemus He says that it is necessary to be born again, and that without such spiritual regeneration it is impossible to enter and experience the kingdom of God. In turning to Him, we find Him, and undergo a fundamental change of nature, from which point we may experience God on a daily basis, should we choose to walk with Him.

The experience of God furnishes all the personal proof that we could ever require as a basis of faith. We do not need to have an experience of God in order to believe in

Him at the level of mental assent, but we do need to prove His existence for ourselves if we are going to know Him personally and walk with Him from day to day.

Mere mental assent to the proposition that God exists is not enough. But if it results in a person turning to Him, and being born again, then it has fulfilled its purpose. For those who seek God will find Him. Wherever people turn to Him from the heart, He makes Himself known to them. As Moses says:

> ...you will seek the LORD your God, and you will find Him if you seek Him with all your heart and with all your soul.   Deuteronomy 4:29

David, the psalmist agrees:

> Taste and see that the Lord is good; blessed is the man who trusts in Him!   Psalm 34:8

We may come to God simply on the basis of our search for Him, but when we find Him, we receive the faith of God, a knowing that He is. The discovery of God is the beginning of the faith of the heart, and the more we receive from Him, the more we trust in Him. This is the faith that Paul writes of when he says:

> Faith comes by hearing, and hearing by the word of God.   Romans 10:17

To discover God for the first time, we need only seek Him, but to come regularly and to walk with Him daily we must have faith, which is why the writer of Hebrews says:

But without faith it is impossible to please Him, for he who comes to God must believe that He is, and that He is a rewarder of those who diligently seek Him.
Hebrews 11:6

The King of Heaven is calling you.

Praise, my soul, the King of Heaven,
To His feet thy tribute bring;
Ransomed, healed, restored, forgiven,
Who like me His praise should sing?
Alleluia! Alleluia!
Praise the everlasting King.

Praise Him for His grace and favour
To our fathers in distress;
Praise Him still the same as ever,
Slow to chide, and swift to bless:
Alleluia! Alleluia!
Glorious in His faithfulness.

Father-like, He tends and spares us
Well our feeble frame He knows;
In His hands He gently bears us,
Rescues us from all our foes:
Alleluia! Alleluia!
Widely as His mercy flows.

Angels, help us to adore Him;
Ye behold Him face to face;
Sun and moon, bow down before Him,
Dwellers all in time and space:
Alleluia! Alleluia!
Praise with us the God of grace.

Henry F. Lyte, 1834

III
ONE THING

Some view seeking God as a luxury rather than a necessity, the sort of thing one might do as a kind of hobby, once one has done everything else one needs to do. Needless to say, such a view, like those who hold it, could not be further from the truth.

Becoming the best you can be is impossible without spiritual regeneration and inspiration. Hearing from Heaven is absolutely fundamental to the abundant life of both individuals and groups. There's neither a day, nor a moment, in which it is irrelevant to hear from above. Far from being the last thing on our personal agenda, attending to Heaven and its business should be at the head of our priorities, our first concern.

There is no greater necessity than that of divine inspiration. Where Heaven is followed, all things are influenced for good, but where the Way of Heaven is rejected, evil triumphs.

As one might expect, Jesus prioritised divine inspiration in His teaching. Indeed, it was His first message when He began to preach:

Repent, for the kingdom of Heaven is at hand.
Matthew 4:17

This was also the message of John the Baptist, as he prepared the way for Christ. John and Jesus were both saying that the best thing anyone could do was to change their perspective, away from the earthly, towards Heaven and its King.

Heaven for these preachers was not simply a destination for the righteous dead, but an ever present resource for the living. The life and assistance of Heaven was available now. Its King was present on earth, and ready to receive all who would come to Him. The Kingdom of Heaven was truly at hand, and still is.

Throughout His earthly ministry, Christ stressed the primary foundational importance of inspiration. For example, when responding to the complaints of His friend Martha, over her sister Mary's failure to help her with the preparations for a meal, Jesus recognised Martha's hard work, but made it very clear that in choosing to sit at His feet and listen, Mary had made the better choice. He says to Martha:

> *Martha, Martha, you are worried and troubled about many things. But one thing is needed, and Mary has chosen that good part, which will not be taken away from her.* Luke 10:41&42

In any, and every, human life, one thing is needed above all others: to sit at the feet of Jesus and listen to Him. Seeking God is the single most valuable thing that any of us can do.

What has the prior place in your life? Is it the busyness of the day, or the business of eternity? Both are important, but to get them in the wrong order of priority is, as we say, to put the cart before the horse. Christ championed the primacy of inspiration over perspiration. If hard work is valuable, meditation is more so. And where there is no inspiration, work has no value!

That revelation is the foundation for right living is at the heart of Christ's message. When Simon Peter recognises that Jesus really is the Christ, Jesus points out that this was not something he arrived at by human reason or education. He says:

> *Blessed are you, Simon Bar-Jonah, for flesh and blood has not revealed this to you, but My Father who is in Heaven.* Matthew 16:17

He then explains to him that, *"On this rock,"* the foundation of revelation, *"I will build My church"* (*Matthew 16:18*). There is only one sure foundation – the word of God.

Again and again in His preaching and teaching, Christ stressed through parable and precept, the need to hear from Heaven. Even before His ministry began, He strongly affirmed this central principle, when He said, to the devil, during His temptation in the wilderness:

Man shall not live by bread alone, but by every word that proceeds from the mouth of God.

Matthew 4:4

Whether we face threats or opportunities, safety or danger, comfort or difficulty, our question should always be, "What does God say about it?"

Divine inspiration is our primary need, as Jesus taught so often during His earthly life. To the tempter He says, *"Man shall not live by bread alone" (Matthew 4:4)*. To the woman at the well He says, *"Whoever drinks of this water will thirst again, but whoever drinks of the water that I shall give him will never thirst. But the water that I shall give him will become in him a fountain of water springing up into everlasting life" (John 4:13,14)*. To the people at the feast He says, *"If anyone thirsts, let him come to Me and drink. He who believes in Me, as the Scripture has said, out of his heart will flow rivers of living water" (John 7:37,38)*.

There is no substitute for divine inspiration. It is unique. With it, works of lasting value are created. Without it, there is only rubbish. This is why Saint Paul, in the first of his letters to followers of The Way at Corinth, emphasises the need for care in how we approach our work:

For we are God's fellow workers; you are God's field, you are God's building. According to the grace of God which was given to me, as a wise master builder I have laid the foundation, and another builds on it. But let each one take heed how he builds on it. For no other foundation can anyone lay than that which is laid, which is Jesus Christ. Now if anyone builds on this foundation with gold, silver, precious stones, wood, hay, straw, each one's work will become clear; for the Day will declare it, because it will be revealed by fire; and the fire will test each one's work, of what sort it is. If anyone's work which he has built on it endures, he will receive a reward. If anyone's work is burned, he will suffer loss; but he himself will be saved, yet so as through fire.

I Corinthians 3:9-15

Idle words and eternally worthless actions are the fruit of a life lived without God's counsel. They are like wood, hay, and stubble — easily combustible materials, utterly unable to withstand the fire of God that will ultimately test all things. In contrast, words and actions born out of a life spent seeking God, are like gold and precious stones, their substance indestructible and their value eternal. All those who say and do such things will be rewarded by Heaven.

Heaven invites us to act as its ambassadors on earth, but how can we represent a kingdom that we do not know? How can we properly serve a king whose voice we do not hear? The King calls us to His throne, but do we heed the call?

Come to Me, all you who labour and are heavy laden, and I will give you rest. Take My yoke upon you and learn from Me, for I am gentle and lowly in heart, and you will find rest for your souls. For My yoke is easy and My burden is light.

Matthew 11:28-30

Whosoever will may come, for the invitation is to all, and everyone who comes is, in that very moment, born of Heaven.

IV
REBIRTH

The capacity to be inspired is not enough. Everyone has that capacity, but not everyone hears from Heaven. The ability to see with the mind's eye and to hear with the inner ear no more guarantees that we will use these faculties to connect with God, than ownership of a telephone determines who we will call. From the start a choice must be made. When it comes to inspiration, the choice is yours. You choose your muse.

Many and varied are the choices people make in this respect. Material and financial wealth, ambition and achievement, power and influence, social acceptance and status, are just a few of the great many goals that inspire those who adopt them. Whatever the perceived value of such sources may be, people ask too much when they make any one of these their primary source of inspiration, their guiding purpose. Why? — Because they are temporal and limited in nature. For this reason the psalmist says:

Some trust in chariots, and some in horses; but we will remember the name of the Lord our God.

Psalm 20:7

If you would experience and enjoy divine inspiration on a daily basis, there is only one place to go: Deity. He has come as far as He can to you, and stands at the very door of your heart, but you must let Him in. He says:

Behold, I stand at the door and knock. If anyone hears My voice and opens the door, I will come in to him and dine with him, and he with Me. To him who overcomes I will grant to sit with Me on My throne, as I also overcame and sat down with My Father on His throne. He who has an ear, let him hear what the Spirit says to the churches. Revelation 3:20-22

Here, in this place of inner fellowship with Christ, abundant inspiration will be found. The divinely inspired life is one of continual turning to God.

Divine inspiration is the fruit of divine relationship. The Holy Spirit is waiting to inspire you. He has much to say to you. But you must come into relationship with God – there is no other way.

If you have never taken this step of opening the door of your heart to God, and letting Him in, I invite you to take it now. It's a simple matter of making friends. Just tell Him that you are opening the door and welcoming Him into your heart and life as your Lord and Saviour. Here is an example of the kind of prayer you might pray:

Heavenly Father, thank you for giving your Son, Jesus Christ, to suffer death on a cross, carrying my sins, and paying the penalty I deserved. I turn from my sin, and I receive you Jesus as my Saviour, my Lord, and my friend. Come into my heart now, and fill me with your Holy Spirit. I put my full trust in you, and I will seek you every day of my life. Thank you for saving me from my sin, and for giving me the free gift of eternal life. I will love you and serve you forever. Amen.

V
HEAVEN'S CITIZENS

If you prayed the prayer at the end of the previous chapter, or one like it, your new life has begun. You have been spiritually reborn. That's how Jesus describes the moment we come to God and put our faith in Him. In His conversation with Nicodemus, a Jewish ruler, He spoke of the need to be born again, and of how it was impossible to see the kingdom of God unless one was. To daily experience this kingdom one must be born into it.

None can see Heaven, unless they are born there. This is why Jesus says, *"You must be born again" (John 3:7).* Unless one is born of the Spirit, one cannot see the kingdom of God. In the instant that we come to Him, entrusting our life to Him, we are spiritually reborn. Now we are citizens of Heaven, resident on earth.

As Heaven's citizens, we no longer walk merely in the light of earthly wisdom, for now our life is *"hidden with Christ in God" (Colossians 3:3).* Although physically present on earth, we are spiritually present in Heaven:

But God, who is rich in mercy, because of His great love with which He loved us, even when we were dead in trespasses, made us alive together with Christ (by grace you have been saved), and raised us up together, and made us sit together in the heavenly places in Christ

Jesus, that in the ages to come He might show the exceeding riches of His grace in His kindness toward us in Christ Jesus. For by grace you have been saved through faith, and that not of yourselves; it is the gift of God, not of works, lest anyone should boast. For we are His workmanship, created in Christ Jesus for good works, which God prepared beforehand that we should walk in them.   *Ephesians 2:4-10*

Now you are seated with Christ in Heaven. At this time, your presence in Heaven is spiritual rather than physical. Christ is physically present in Heaven, but spiritually present both in Heaven and on earth. In contrast, you are physically present on earth, but spiritually present both on earth and in Heaven.

You are no longer the person you were, for your nature has been changed. You are *"a new creation" (2 Corinthians 5:17),* a regenerated being, a child of God, but like any newborn baby, you have now embarked upon the developmental journey of your new life.

You have a new heavenly nature, similar to that of Christ, which is why John says, *"As He is, so are we in this world" (1 John 4:17).* But unlike Christ, whose character is already perfect, your nature must be developed. As Paul explains, this is a path of growth:

But we all, with unveiled face, beholding as in a mirror the glory of the Lord, are being transformed into the same image from glory to glory, just as by the Spirit of the Lord.   *2 Corinthians 3:18*

Whoever spends time with God becomes like Him. It is as you behold Him that you are transformed, so this is where you must direct your attention. Your new life is to be lived...

Looking unto Jesus, the author and finisher of our faith, who for the joy that was set before Him endured the cross, despising the shame, and has sat down at the right hand of the throne of God.   *Hebrews 12:2*

VI
LISTEN

Through the second birth, we enter a personal relationship with God in which it is possible, indeed natural, for us to see and hear spiritual things. Our life of divine inspiration begins here, but like all relationships, it must be cultivated.

Just as a good human parent cares for their child from the moment of birth, our heavenly Father seeks to nurture us from the start. He's not interested in a distant relationship, but a friendship characterised by love and trust. We should therefore seek Him from the beginning, just as a baby seeks the succour and security of its human parents.

We must go to God. The psalmist says:

Be still, and know that I am God.   Psalm 46:10a

Habakkuk says:

I will stand my watch and set myself on the rampart, and watch to see what He will say to me.   Habakkuk 2:1

If we would live our lives to the full, we must be obedient to Heaven. We cannot be obedient unless we hear, we cannot hear unless we listen, and we cannot listen unless we come to Him in stillness. This is the way, the only way.

It is important to stress that the stillness of which we speak is internal, rather than external. There may be times, especially at the beginning, when one is starting to learn to listen to God, when it is easier to still the mind if one is in a quiet and peaceful place. But such a setting, although desirable, is by no means necessary for seeking God. In fact, it may be better to learn this stillness in the midst of noise, as we will often be required to maintain it in busy or inharmonious places.

I am reminded of the story of a man who, many centuries ago, went to the Abbott of a monastery in the Egyptian desert, and asked to be admitted to the monastic order so that he might learn to seek God in stillness. The Abbott was willing to admit him, but pointed out to him that this was not the highest way. If he wanted that, he must go to the crowded markets of Alexandria and learn to hear God there!

Without seeking God there is no divine inspiration. Walking with God is about seeking Him. It's an action of the heart, something we do within ourselves, which is why David wrote:

> *When You said, "Seek My face," my heart said to You, "Your face, Lord, I will seek"*   *Psalm 27:8*

Although originally spoken to a specific group of people who had been taken into exile, God's words communicated through the prophet Jeremiah, are as relevant to us today as they were to the captives to whom they were addressed:

> *For I know the thoughts that I think toward you, says the Lord, thoughts of peace and not of evil, to give you a future and a hope. Then you will call upon Me and go and pray to Me, and I will listen to you. And you will seek Me and find Me, when you search for Me with all your heart. I will be found by you, says the Lord.*
> *Jeremiah 29:11-14a*

Anyone can learn to seek God. It's simple, so easy that a child can do it. And when we seek Him, we find Him. Some expression of inspiration is always the outcome, if we persevere.

But although the act of seeking God is itself relatively straightforward, learning to seek God on a regular basis, so that we do so habitually and automatically requires diligent practice. Let's take a closer look at this process.

Seeking God starts with stilling the soul. He says to us:

> *Be still, and know that I am God; I will be exalted among the nations, I will be exalted in the earth!*
> *Psalm 46:10*

Stillness is not something you turn on. It's something you experience when the usual concerns of your mind are turned off. Generally speaking, you are less likely to hear from God if your mind is preoccupied by other things.

Stillness is achieved by putting aside our own thoughts, so that we may experience the thoughts of God. We lay aside our concerns, temporarily quieting our own inner voice, so that we may hear the voice of God within us.

It's important to stress that this is not a total suspension of mental activity. The aim is not to turn off all thought, completely blanking or emptying the mind. Whilst this might be a characteristic of some practices that go under the name of meditation, it is utterly foreign to the ancient practice of seeking God. In fact, it is antithetical to it, for such a blank mind will prove as dead to God as it is to its own thoughts! God is not looking for empty minds and mindless servants, but for co-workers, friends who talk together with Him, and who come to agreement through inspiration and conviction, not through domination and coercion.

In stillness we make room for God. We turn down the volume of our inner world, so that His voice may be heard. We pull our attention back from all else that would claim it, and in so doing we prepare to hear from Heaven.

Just as stillness, or silence, is a turning away from our usual concerns, so seeking God is a turning towards Him. We pull the mind away from every other focus, and direct our attention to Him. We imagine Him, we picture Him.

Whether you have recently come to know God, or you have known Him for some time, try this simple exercise. If possible, find a quiet spot where you are not likely to be disturbed. Sit comfortably, take a few deep breaths, and seek to relax. In suggesting these preliminaries, I do so with the important caveat that, as we have seen, they are by no means vital to seeking God, but that they may help, especially at the beginning, when one is first learning to overcome distractions, still the mind, and listen to Him. What *is* vital is to be still, for it is in stillness that God is known.

Quieten your mind, laying aside its usual concerns, in order to focus your attention on God. With repeated practice you will get better and better at creating the right internal attitude to seek Him. In fact, after a while, getting to that place where you can hear from Heaven will become something you can do very quickly indeed. But at the beginning, you will need to practice taking control of your mind and focusing it on Him.

Be still and picture God in your mind. "But what does He look like?" you might ask. Thankfully, God has helped us in this by taking our humanity upon Himself and living on earth as a man.

When Philip the disciple asked Jesus to show them the Father, He said:

Have I been with you so long, and yet you have not known Me, Philip? He who has seen Me has seen the Father; so how can you say, 'Show us the Father'? Do you not believe that I am in the Father, and the Father in Me? The words that I speak to you I do not speak on

*My own authority; but the Father who dwells in Me
does the works. Believe Me that I am in the Father and
the Father in Me.*   John 14:9-11

Christ was repeating His earlier assertion, made in response
to demands from the Jews to tell them plainly who He was,
when He had said, *"I and My Father are one"* (John 10:30).
As John says at the start of his gospel:

*No one has seen God at any time. The only begotten
Son, who is in the bosom of the Father, He has declared
Him.*   John 1:18

For this reason, we need only to picture the Lord Jesus
Christ present with us, just as He promised He would be,
when He said, *"I am with you always, even to the end of the
age"* (Matthew 28:20). The writer of Hebrews talks of:

Looking unto Jesus, the author and finisher of our faith
                                                     Hebrews 12:2

Whilst it is perfectly good and right to picture any member
of the Trinity, or even the Trinity as a whole, it is so easy to
look to Jesus that even a small child may do it.

Hearing from Heaven is an active rather than a passive
event. We do not still our hearts, simply to wait passively
until God should communicate with us, but rather we
actively seek Him. Our waiting is active, not passive. We

make a deliberate and conscious choice to attend to Heaven. It is necessary to actively look to God, just as you might actively scan the physical landscape in order to pick out a particular person or object. If you seek God you will find Him. The opposite is also true: if you don't, you won't.

You have focused your mind on God. You have pictured Him with you. Now imagine Him speaking to you. What does He say?

As you listen, test what you hear with your spirit. Does your spirit witness to the truth of it? If it does, make a mental or written note of what you hear. No other messages you receive will be as important as those from Heaven. If it doesn't, go back to God and listen again. Keep doing this, until you receive a word that witnesses with your spirit.

As you focus your attention on God in this way, be open to whatever you may receive from Heaven. For example, there may be times when God has things to say to us that we may not like, or that run counter to our expectations. We may not always like what God says, and we may sometimes be surprised or challenged by what He says, but we will always be wise to follow what He says.

Be open to whatever He might show you. By adopting an attitude of radical openness to Heaven, you optimise your ability to hear, and you put yourself in a place where, should you be unable to hear by virtue of your psychological defences, God will somehow find a way around these in order to get His message through to you.

Finally, make a not in your diary to start each and every day in this manner. Make seeking God the first thing you do each morning. There's no better way to begin each day than to set your heart on Heaven.

Peace, perfect peace, in this dark world of sin?
The blood of Jesus whispers peace within.

Peace, perfect peace, by thronging duties pressed?
To do the will of Jesus, this is rest.

Peace, perfect peace, with sorrow surging round?
In Jesus's presence nought but calm is found.

Peace, perfect peace, with loved ones far away?
In Jesus's keeping we are safe, and they.

Peace, perfect peace, our future all unknown?
Jesus we know, and He is on the throne.

Peace, perfect peace, death shadowing us and ours?
Jesus has vanquished death and all its powers.

It is enough: earth's struggles soon shall cease,
And Jesus call us to Heaven's perfect peace.

Edward Bickersteth, 1875

VII
HOLY MEDIA

When we find God, we discover that He is a God of surprises, a being of boundless creativity, whose works express infinite variety, and whose words are communicated through an immense variety of different media.

Adopt a limited view of the Almighty and you greatly limit yourself. Rather, expect the unexpected.

Be open to hearing from God by whatever means He would use to communicate with you. God will certainly make Himself known to you, but this may involve any or all of the inner sensory modalities. Whilst language is a primary medium for clear communication, it is not the only way in which God speaks. You may see visions, be touched by God, taste flavours, smell fragrances, or simply experience a spiritual sense that a thing is so, a moving or prompting of your spirit. Be open to receiving from Heaven in any way that God should choose.

Divine illumination is essentially a message from Heaven to the human heart, but that message can come through a wide range of means, and in this chapter we'll look at some of these.

Whatever the channel through which it comes to us, God's word carries and applies His creative power. This is the word by which the universe was made.

God *spoke* creation into being:

Then God said, "Let there be light"; and there was light.
Genesis 1:3

By faith we understand that the worlds were framed by the word of God, so that the things which are seen were not made of things which are visible.
Hebrews 11:3

Every time you hear from God, and take that word to heart, His creative power, the same power that made the universe, is applied to your life! That power will work both within you and around you. Within you there will be many wonderful consequences, as your character becomes increasingly like His. You will become more and more benevolent, as His love fills and overflows your heart. Your faith will grow stronger and stronger, until it is established like granite. Your wisdom will deepen with every word you receive from Heaven. And your works, whatever they are, will be outstanding in Heaven's sight, for the divine power of which we speak is not restricted to the transformation of your inner self, but radiates invisibly yet gloriously around you with an immeasurable impact for good. This is the inevitable outcome of your diligence in seeking God, and His faithfulness in answering you.

THE WITNESS OF THE SPIRIT

Whenever God speaks to us personally, the Holy Spirit is involved. He speaks to us through the witness of His Spirit to our spirit. Saint Paul describes this in relation to God assuring us that we are His children, when he says:

> *The Spirit Himself bears witness with our spirit that we are the children of God.*   *Romans 8:16*

Although used here to communicate the greatest fact regarding our relationship with God, the witness of the Spirit may be experienced in relation to any truth that we need to know, or direction that we need to take. Saint John says:

> *And it is the Spirit who bears witness because the Spirit is truth ... He who believes in the Son of God has the witness in Himself.*   *I John 5,6&10*

The Holy Spirit is an inner witness of the truth to our heart. His influence upon us may be direct, unmediated by any vehicle other than Himself, or it may be conveyed via many different channels. But though His dress may differ, the quality and character of His witness are constant.

When we talk about the direct influence of the Spirit, we do so under the great limitation that the direct communications of the Spirit cannot be adequately expressed in human language. Words may be used to describe the message brought, but they cannot properly describe the experience itself.

The witness of the Holy Spirit to our spirit may be experienced as an inner knowing or certain conviction that a thing is so. Alternatively, it may be experienced as a sense in our spirit, the meaning or significance of which we may not understand, as when God is alerting us to something, and we need to stop and seek Him as to what it means. A further possibility is when we experience being prompted to act, or not act, in a certain way, such as when we experience either a sense of warning in relation to something, or the opposite sense that a given step or path is the right one.

This witness of the Spirit may be conveyed via a range of different media. It may come through prayer, through the reading of scripture, through an audible or inner voice, through visions, through dreams, through an experience of the natural world, through thoughts, through feelings, or through any other channel, or combination of channels, that God may use.

PRAYER

Prayer is the primary medium of spiritual communication, the essential connection with Heaven.

To say that we hear God through prayer is to state the obvious, but only for those who see it as a two-way communication. For those who see prayer as merely a one-way link, through which we talk to God but do not expect Him to communicate with us, there is no personal comfort, insight, or direction from Heaven.

Prayer is communication with God. Put simply, we talk to Him, and He listens to us; He talks to us, and we listen to Him. Of course, by talk, we mean a lot more than just speaking words. We are referring to everything we express to God and that He extends to us. We communicate our attitudes, our faith, our doubts, our thoughts, our motives, our feelings, and our actions. God communicates His life, His love, His faith, His strength, His truth, His plans, His wisdom, His guidance, and so much more.

Saint Paul not only encourages prayer, but continual prayer. *"Pray without ceasing,"* he says (I Thessalonians 5:17), knowing that unbroken communion is the fruit of constant prayer. In a later chapter we will see how unbroken communion becomes the experience of those who diligently follow the Way of Heaven.

SACRED TEXTS

God speaks to us through scriptures, that is, writings inspired by the Holy Spirit. Their message may be read and understood by anyone with a desire to hear from Heaven and follow its Way.

Saint Paul summarises the value of scripture:

All Scripture is given by inspiration of God, and is profitable for doctrine, for reproof, for correction, for instruction in righteousness, that the man of God may be complete, thoroughly equipped for every good work.
2 Timothy 3:16&17

There are two aspects to interpreting sacred texts: the universal and the personal. If we read scripture as we would read any other book, we may learn a great deal that is of value both to ourselves and others. Any and all may read in this way, which is why we describe it as the universal aspect. But when we read scripture in the conscious presence of its Author, not simply thinking about the words that we are reading, but listening to God as He interprets those words to us, we move from the universal to the personal. Now God is speaking to us directly and individually through the written words He inspired. When scripture is read in such an attitude of prayer, God may speak to us personally through any text He chooses, with a specific word that we need to hear at that moment in time.

Try this for yourself. Open your Bible, select a verse, and ask God to speak to you through it. Wait on Him, and note what He says to you.

AN INNER OR AUDIBLE VOICE

It is natural for those who listen to God, to hear His voice. He speaks both to those who do not know Him, revealing Himself and calling them into relationship with Him, and He speaks daily with those who follow Him, directing them in the Way of Heaven. Jesus said:

> *My sheep hear My voice, and I know them, and they follow Me.* John 10:27

This communication via language is mostly an inner experience. Although it is possible for God to speak to us in an audible voice, it is more usually the case that His voice is heard inwardly and privately.

There may be occasions when God gives us a message for another person or group. This is prophecy. If you believe that you have received such a message, it is most important that you do everything within your power to ensure that this really is a message from Heaven, and not merely your own imagination, or a demonic deception. Whilst true prophetic messages from Heaven can achieve very great good, false messages can cause a great deal of harm. If you are experienced in listening to God, it is less likely that you will make a mistake of this kind, but it is always a possibility, however spiritually mature you may be. For this reason, we should take great care when it comes to sharing prophetic words with others. If we have the witness of the Holy Spirit that this is a word for them, then it is our responsibility to share it, and to do so in the way Heaven directs. Let God guide you in when and how to share.

VISIONS AND DREAMS

There are times when God speaks through visions and dreams.

> *And it shall come to pass in the last days, says God, that I will pour out of My Spirit on all flesh; your sons and your daughters shall prophesy, your young men shall see visions, your old men shall dream dreams.*
>
> *Acts 2:17*

Visions may involve our external senses, or they may be wholly internal. Saint Paul wrote of receiving an abundance of such revelations.

Dreams may also be revelatory. Although it might be argued that every dream has significance for the dreamer, it is not the case that all dreams are direct messages from Heaven. Those that are often possess a quality of greater lifelikeness or reality.

VIII
IMAGINATION TO ILLUMINATION

What role, if any, does the imagination play in taking the Way of Heaven? Much depends on the use we make of it. If imagination is understood as being the construction of ideas, images, sounds, and other experiences within ourselves, it will prove a helpful tool for seeking God, but not necessarily for hearing Him. Let's take a closer look at the role of imagination in each of these activities.

As we have seen, to seek God is to actively attend to Him. Because God is not visible to the physical eye, this necessarily entails the deliberate use of the imagination. Imagination can help us to consciously draw near to God. By picturing Him with us, visualising Heaven, or imagining that He speaks with us, we are reaching out to God, moving towards Him, and getting ready to receive from Heaven. Used in this way, imagination can help us focus on God and connect with Him.

I have often suggested to people that they imagine God speaking to them personally, as this opens the way to hearing from Heaven. Just as you might picture someone known to you, but not physically present with you, and imagine them speaking to you, so you may picture Christ in your mind, and imagine Him talking with you. But that's where the similarity ends. Imagination is used in each case, but there is a significant difference between imagining that you are talking with another human being, and imagining that you are talking with God. In the first instance, you are imagining the words of someone who is not there, but in the second, you are using your inner senses to 'picture' One who is always with you, wherever you are. The object of your imagination is actually there. So we might conclude that the use of the imagination may help us discern the Lord and His heavenly kingdom.

But how helpful is imagination in hearing God? In turning to God we may find it helpful to remember that He is with us, and to picture Him, but having found Him, we must allow Him to say whatever He would to us rather than what we think He will, or should, say. We move therefore from imagining to listening. This is a vital transition, for if we only imagine, we may erroneously imagine all kinds of things, and fall into many serious errors of judgement and action.

The principle here is well illustrated by the following response of a child learning to listen to God for the first time. Having simply yet clearly explained how to do it, the parent invites the child to listen. "What do you hear God say?" asks the parent. "God says you should take me to the toyshop and buy me whatever I want!" replies the child. Although this might be what God is saying, it is more likely that the child is projecting his or her own desires on to Him.

Rather than imagining God saying what we would like Him to say, or even what we fear, we still our imagination, and in the stillness we listen for whatever He would say to us. So it is that through the active use of the imagination we may arrive at the Way of Heaven, but having arrived, we subjugate our imagination to what we hear by our inner ear and what we see by our inner eye. Imagination primes the pump, but only God can deliver the living water.

How do we know that we have made this transition? How can we be sure that we are really talking with Him, and not simply imagining the whole thing? To answer this, we must enter the realm of the spirit.

You are a spirit. Spirit is your essential nature, the 'you' that is born again when you come to God through faith in Christ. Prior to the second birth, you are unable to discern heavenly things. Knowing only the first birth, your spirit is dead to God. But after the second birth, your inner eyes and ears are opened to God and His kingdom. Now you have the spiritual ability to discern between truth and falsehood, right and wrong, God and the devil. Like an infant learning to walk, you must develop this ability through practice, but should you choose to exercise it, your ability to discern God will grow stronger and stronger with each passing day.

So, to answer the question of how one may be sure that one is hearing from God, growing spiritual discernment is the key. The Holy Spirit witnesses truth to our spirit, so that we know what to accept and what to reject.

Solomon says:

*The spirit of a man is the lamp of the Lord, searching
all the inner depths of his heart.*

Proverbs 20:27

Your spirit is God's light within you. It's as though He
turns the light on inside you, enabling you to see things as
they really are, should you choose to.

If you follow it, you will find that this inner witness is
supremely reliable, having its origin in God. This is a kind
of knowing far deeper than that of the discursive intellect, a
knowing that carries a quality of conviction that a thing is
so.

Because this knowledge comes from the spirit, there may
be times when it defies logical explanation. This is not the
same thing as saying that it is illogical. Were we to possess
all information and all wisdom in relation to any matter, we
would readily acknowledge the logic of God's guidance in it.
But from where we stand, this logic may not always be
apparent. The conclusions of our limited reason and
research will not always concur with revelation. God reveals
truth to those who will turn to Him and listen. The wise
accept that truth and follow it, knowing that, *"Wisdom is
justified by all her children"* (Luke 7:35). The evidence will
ultimately show that they were right.

IX
TEST EVERYTHING

The New Testament book of Acts records the wise response of the first century residents of Berea to the preaching of Paul and Silas, leading missionaries of the early church. When they heard Paul and Silas speak, these people did not unquestioningly accept everything they heard, but they, *"Searched the Scriptures daily to find out whether these things were so" (Acts 17:11)*.

It is important to test what we hear. Paul says, *"Test all things" (1 Thessalonians 5:21)*. The witness of the Holy Spirit to our spirit is a fundamental test, for only spirit can discern spiritual things. Your mind must become the servant of your regenerate spirit. Sadly, some who are born again subjugate the spirit to the mind, and so deny themselves the walk with God that they might have had.

To be consistently led by the Holy Spirit is something that is learnt by practice over a period of time. By always testing what we hear, we grow better at identifying its source. As you seek God each day, use your spiritual discernment to judge what you hear. Practice identifying where it originated. Is it from God? Is it an expression of your own mind, such as your wishes or your fears? Is it of demonic origin? Is it the internalised voice of someone known to you, such as a father or mother, a sister or brother, a friend or foe, a teacher or other authority figure?

If you get into the habit of testing what you hear, you will in time develop the ability to quickly discern the voice of God.

But even when you have learnt to distinguish reliably between voices, you must still continue to judge. The fact that you have developed competence in a skill doesn't mean that you can stop making an effort to do your best, or that you no longer need to check the standard of your work. Testing what you hear is always necessary. However great your experience, you must still be careful, for, as Peter warns, there is an ever present danger:

> *Be sober, be vigilant, because your adversary the devil walks about like a roaring lion, seeking whom he may devour.* *I Peter 5:8*

Remember that you have a deadly enemy, an adversary who will attempt to trick you on occasions, if necessary even by impersonating the voice of God,

> *For Satan himself transforms himself into an angel of light.* *2 Corinthians 11:14*

With practice you will develop growing confidence in your ability to discern, but be aware of the dangers of over-confidence. An exaggerated sense of security can lead to a lack of spiritual vigilance and easily result in your being deceived.

The apostle Paul warns:

Let him who thinks he stands, take heed lest he fall.
I Corinthians 10:12

Seek to remain watchful and vigilant at all times. Test everything you hear by submitting it to the judgement of the Holy Spirit, whose mission is to lead you into all truth. Reject everything that fails the test!

X
ORDERS FIRST, MISSION SECOND

The way in which we start each day has a profound influence on the events of that day, the course of our life, and the effects of our life upon the lives of others.

What kind of things do you say to yourself when you awake? What are the first thoughts and feelings that you experience? If you cannot answer this question, put a notebook and a pen by your bed, and when you awake tomorrow, write down your first thoughts and feelings, as many as you can recall.

Next, critically reflect on these. Are they positive or negative, helpful or unhelpful, accurate or inaccurate? Take a moment to consider how these initial thoughts and feelings might influence how you approach the day, your activities during the day, and your experience of the day. Be radically honest with yourself as you appraise the quality of your daily genesis. Beginnings matter. Starting poorly may cost an athlete the race.

Starting well, whether in an occupation, a sport, or a day on earth, is not something people are naturally good at. Good starts have to be learnt. They are acquired by those who diligently practice them, until they become their automatic and unconscious response.

Whatever you may find when you examine your own daily start, ask yourself this question, "How would I like to begin my day?" As before, take a moment to reflect on this and to come up with your answer.

The next step is to improve your daily start. Even if you feel that you generally start the day well, there is usually some room for improvement. Whatever your present situation and whatever challenges you currently face, you will find that the best perspective on any matter, and the greatest power to transform any area, come from Heaven.

Develop the habit of turning to God on waking. At the start, you may need a prompt to jog your memory in this respect. Consider doing something that will help you to remember, such as writing a note and standing it by your alarm clock, so that when you awake and turn off your alarm, you will see the note and be reminded of your resolve.

Don't worry if you miss a day. That's all part of the learning process. What matters is not that you do things perfectly from the beginning (an impossibility!) but that you keep practising, and that you don't stop practising until you have formed the habit of seeking God whenever you wake.

By practising in this way, you are developing the discipline of starting each day in the Way of Heaven. There is no better start to a day on earth, and no greater way of ensuring that what you do has eternal value. Diligent practice is the key. Keep practicing and you will surely develop this habit.

The time to start listening to God is the moment you wake. God alone knows what you need to hear at the start of each new day. He is ready to brief you, so that you will enter the day informed and prepared. To enter the day without this briefing is madness and folly. Only an idiot of the first order refuses the support of One who knows all things, and has the power to help you fully accomplish your mission.

Whilst it is good to seek God from the moment you wake, it is wise to make allowance for the fact that you may be somewhat sleepy, having just woken, and your concentration therefore may not yet be at its best. Because of this, it may be a good idea to have a specific time when you are fully awake, to specifically seek God's directions for the day. This doesn't obviate the need to seek Him on waking (it's never too soon to start chatting with God!), but it does mean that you are more likely to retain important information from Heaven. When you are sufficiently awake to concentrate properly, you will be more likely to remember what is said to you.

Ask God to tell you what you need to know. He will. Ask Him also to tell you what He wants you to do that day. God has a great plan, conceived in eternity, and you are part of that plan. Long before your birth, God prepared a way for you to walk in, and valuable work for you to do. There is only one way you can fulfil your heavenly mission and complete your great works and that is by walking with God. As you take your orders from Him each day and obey them, you will surely complete the work that God has given you to do.

Forth in Thy name, O Lord, I go,
My daily labour to pursue,
Thee, only Thee, resolved to know
In all I think, or speak, or do.

The task Thy wisdom has assigned
O let me cheerfully fulfil;
In all my works Thy presence find,
And prove Thy good and perfect will.

Thee may I set at my right hand,
Whose eyes my inmost substance see;
And labour on at Thy command,
And offer all my works to Thee.

Give me to bear Thy easy yoke,
And every moment watch and pray,
And still to things eternal look,
And hasten to Thy glorious day.

For Thee delightfully employ
Whate'er Thy bounteous grace hath given,
And run my course with even joy,
And closely walk with Thee to Heaven.

Charles Wesley, 1749

XI
THE INNER KINGDOM

Divine inspiration is for everyone. No one need be without it, though sadly there have been many who have lived in the darkness of its absence.

Not only is it for all, it is available everywhere on earth. Wherever you are, wherever you go, inspiration is there already, waiting to be found. It has to be, for God is its source. Being omnipresent (everywhere at once), God is with us all. But, like other aspects of our environment, we may or may not attend to Him. Should we, at any time, turn and look to God, we will find Him. Whoever you are and wherever you are, you have only to seek and you shall find.

In describing the act of seeking God in this way, I am using the language of the physical senses to describe an inner perception rather than an external event. However, we know that there are times when God reveals Himself physically and externally. Christ was Himself God incarnate in human flesh. He was seen, He was heard, and He was touched. God spoke to Moses from a real bush that burned, yet was not consumed. He wrote with His finger on Belshazzar's palace wall, words of judgement that were visible to all, and, once interpreted, clearly understood. He spoke audibly to the child Samuel as he slept in the temple. These are just a few examples. History records many other instances of God communicating with humanity through the external physical world, a world that is, in itself, clear evidence of its Creator's hand. But it is not experiences such as these that we are referring to when we talk of seeking God. Rather, we are describing an experience that is essentially inner rather than outer, a true perception of reality, but not that of an external physical object.

Amongst His many teachings on the kingdom of God, Christ made clear that although it has its own independent existence, this kingdom is to be found inside us. He said:

The kingdom of God is within you.   *Luke 17:21*

This is good news, in that we do not need to make a physical journey in order to advance spiritually. The entrance to the kingdom is within us. The way is inner, not outer, and it is the journey of a single step.

However valuable it might be to make a physical pilgrimage, any such quest will be entirely void of spiritual profit, unless and until it is accompanied by the pilgrimage within, for it is within the soul that the wellsprings of life are to be found. This is why Solomon says:

Keep your heart with all diligence, for out of it spring the issues of life.   *Proverbs 4:23*

Whoever would enjoy abundant overflowing life must open their heart to God. This is the step of trust by which we enter the inner kingdom. It is the action of seeking God from the heart.

To look to God is to look with the inner eye, the mind's eye. To listen to God is to listen with the inner ear. It's the same mechanism that you use when you visualise something in your mind.

All of the physical sense modalities have an inner register, so that it is possible to experience the sensation of sight, of sound, of smell, of taste, and of touch, without the stimulation of these physical senses by external physical objects. This faculty extends our experience beyond the limits of what may be known at any moment in time through our physical senses alone. Whether we are picturing an expected future outcome, or remembering a past event, the capacity for inner experience makes it possible. It is this capacity that enables us to see and know God within ourselves. We see Him with the inner eye.

XII
SPIRITUAL DISCERNMENT

If God exists, and it is possible for us to communicate with Him, how do we know whether our experience is valid? Are we hearing from God, or are we deceiving ourselves? If we are hearing Him, how do we know that we are hearing clearly? Are we really hearing from Heaven, or are we misleading ourselves by projecting our own ideas on to Him? In order to answer such questions we must enter the world of training.

Like many other skills, the ability to seek God must be learnt. Skills such as walking, talking, or writing, are not developed without teaching and practice. Hearing God is no exception to this rule. If we are to hear from Heaven, and if we are to do so accurately and consistently, we must be trained. Just as the ear must be trained in music, the eye in art, and the palate for tasting wine, so must the soul be trained to discern the Lord.

It should not be thought that because it is a learnt skill, the ability to reliably seek God is a specialist skill, or that its practice belongs only to prophets, priests, or mystics. Walking, talking, and writing are no more difficult, and they are all learnt by children the world over. How might our world be transformed, were its children taught to seek the Almighty? This is a skill that anyone may learn which is why God says to all, *"Be still, and know that I am God; I* will be exalted among the nations, I will be exalted in the earth!" (Psalm 46:10).

It may be that we know those who have learnt to seek God who can serve as our teachers. Scripture too provides rich guidance on hearing from Heaven. But whether or not we have access to such resources, God Himself will teach us by His Spirit, as we practice. Scripture speaks of,

> *Those who by reason of use have their senses exercised to discern both good and evil.* Hebrews 5:14

Practice is a vital ingredient in this training. It has been said that practice makes perfect, and this is no less true in the matter of seeking God than it is in the development of any other skill. Through diligent practice the seeker becomes increasingly competent in the art of spiritual discernment.

By using their inner senses to regularly seek God, people gradually learn to discriminate between different sources of inner experience. The development of this skill is imperative, as God's voice is not the only voice we may hear within ourselves. Amongst the different inner voices that we may hear are our own inner voice, the internalised voices of others, the voice of God or the voices of angels, and the voice of the devil or the voices of demons. It is only through practice that one learns to reliably identify these different sources, discriminate between them, and so distinguish between good and evil.

As in all training, there is a period during which the skill is being learnt, a period in which mistakes will be made. It has rightly been said that 'the person who never made a mistake, never made anything'. Mistakes, by definition, are not good; no keen student enjoys making them; and some are costly. But, fail we must, if we are to ultimately succeed.

I know a young man who determined to learn to seek God. He practised diligently and began to make progress, but inevitably, he made mistakes. Realising that what he had thought were words from the Lord, were rather projections of his own will, or worse, the tricks of the enemy, he gave up the practice. He still loved God, and he prayed, but he no longer listened. For a time all seemed well, but as the weeks passed, he began to feel increasingly uneasy and troubled within himself. Try as he may, he could not identify the reasons for his lack of peace. Finally, he sought God in prayer, and the Lord spoke to him clearly, saying, "Your peace has gone because you no longer seek Me." Rebuked, he immediately returned to his former discipline of looking to Heaven, and his peace was instantly restored. It was not long before he began to experience the same difficulties as before. "This can't be right," he thought, but instead of pressing on to develop discernment, again he gave up seeking God. His peace of mind soon began to evaporate, and he felt increasingly tense and unhappy. Unable to see the cause of his demise, he prayed to God to show him. "Your peace has gone because you do not seek Me," came the reply. At that point the young man suddenly realised that he must persevere. This time he took up seeking God, never again to lay it down.

If we will persevere in the practice of daily seeking God, we will, in time, become skilled in the art of meditative prayer. This is the training of those who learn to listen to Heaven. It is not hard to understand why this practice is so effective in achieving its aims. If I want to get to know another person, I must spend time with them, talking, listening, and learning. If I am content simply to know about them, it will suffice for me to study their life, learning what I can from available sources. But even if I become an authority on them, so that I know more about them than anyone else, I still do not know them personally. Because of my great knowledge, I may feel that I know them, but still we have never met. We are not even acquaintances, let alone friends. There is no relationship, only data. But if I spend time with someone, I start to get to know them. The more we meet and talk, the better I come to know and understand them. The same principle applies to our relationship with God. The more time we spend with Him, the better we get to know Him, and the less likely we are to confuse Him with someone else. Jesus said,

> *My sheep hear My voice, and I know them, and they follow Me.*   *John 10:27*

Get to know His voice.

XIII
SEEKING GOD IN ADVERSITY

The highest path is rarely the easiest one. History affords many stories of those who sacrificed much to do the work of Heaven and gain the great reward.

The Way of Heaven may be successfully completed by anyone, but all who take it will face difficulties of various kinds. In each danger or crisis, the pilgrim must walk closely and trustingly with Heaven, to overcome. Victory belongs to those who keep the faith, who are not disobedient to their heavenly calling. Whatever the conclusion in terms of outward events, those who trust and obey the King of Heaven are the final conquerors. Their crown cannot be taken away: it is an eternal reward.

Here, by way of example, are two stories about facing adversity. Each deals with events that not only challenged those involved, but threatened their very lives.

The first is from the life of King David, during the time that he was in exile. Having been forced to flee for his life, David had taken refuge with his supporters and their families in Ziklag, a foreign town. For a time all was well, but then disaster struck. One day, whilst David and his men were away from the camp, enemy forces attacked, making off not only with their goods, but also with their wives and children. On their return, David and his troop were devastated to discover their loss. Their initial shock soon turned to anger, and David's men talked of killing him.

What would you do, if you found yourself in a situation like this where not only have you lost everything, but your life is under threat? Adversity, stress, and crisis all test character, and this was a test of the first order. Thankfully, David had been tested many times before, beginning in his youth when he had often rescued his sheep from lions and bears. The best training for adversity is adversity, and David certainly had his share. From early in life he had learnt to look to God in crisis, and had found his way through on each occasion. So when disaster struck, that day in Ziklag, David may not have felt prepared, but God knew that he was ready.

David's response amply proved that this was so, for in that moment when all seemed irrevocably lost, he sought the Lord. David knew that the one thing he needed, above all else, was guidance from Heaven, so to Heaven he turned, and Heaven did not let him down. David inquired of the Lord, saying:

> *"Shall I pursue this troop? Shall I overtake them?" And He answered him, "Pursue, for you shall surely overtake them and without fail recover all."*
>
> *I Samuel 30:8*

When David sought God, God spoke to him, directing him to pursue his enemies, which is exactly what David did.

He gathered his men together, they went in pursuit, and they recovered everything.

Our second story is taken from the life of Moses, during the time that he led his people out of slavery in Egypt. As they approached the Red Sea, Moses realised that the Egyptian army were pursuing them, and that the way ahead was blocked. Ahead lay a sea they could not cross. Behind rode an army they could not conquer. In the face of impending defeat and death, a fearful Moses turned to God for help, and God answered him with a reply that began with a rebuke:

> *And the Lord said to Moses, "Why do you cry to Me? Tell the children of Israel to go forward. But lift up your rod, and stretch out your hand over the sea and divide it. And the children of Israel shall go on dry ground through the midst of the sea."*
>
> *Exodus 14:15&16*

Why did God rebuke Moses on this occasion? God wasn't rebuking Moses for seeking Him — far from it. But He was correcting Moses' understanding of how this crisis situation was to be resolved. That's one of the great things about seeking God. His reply not only gives us the information and direction that we need, but also corrects any misperceptions or misunderstandings that we may have, and which stand in the way of our fulfilling our heavenly destiny. By seeking God, Moses received the divine inspiration that he needed in order to lead his people to safety, and ultimately into the land that God had promised them.

When you next face adversity, as you surely will, take prompt and frequent counsel with the Almighty, for He will make a way. In many cases it will not be easy. In fact, there may be times when it seems to you that all is lost, times when you feel like giving up, or even times when you are tempted to doubt God. At such times stand firm and turn to Him. However fierce the storm, however long the night, He is with you. Consult Him throughout, for He will direct you from Heaven, and in the obedience of faith you will prevail.

He who would valiant be 'gainst all disaster,
Let him in constancy follow the Master.
There's no discouragement shall make him
        once relent
His first avowed intent to be a pilgrim.

Who so beset him round with dismal stories
Do but themselves confound – his strength the
        more is.
No foes shall stay his might; though he with
        giants fight,
He will make good his right to be a pilgrim.

Since, Lord, Thou dost defend us with Thy
        Spirit,
We know we at the end, shall life inherit.
Then fancies flee away! I'll fear not what men
        say,
I'll labour night and day to be a pilgrim.

John Bunyan, 1684

XIV
DESTINATION BY REVELATION

Where is your promised land? Everyone has one. Each has a destination that God would lead them to. That destination is the fulfilment of your divine mission, and the completion of your life's work. No two people share the same calling. Your role is unique, but do you know what it is? If you do, it is only because God has revealed it to you. If you don't, you will only receive it by revelation.

Revelation unlocks. It releases. Jesus said:

If you abide in My word, you are My disciples indeed.
And you shall know the truth, and the truth shall make
you free. John 8:31&32

Whatever the area in which release is needed, revelation will do it. Revelation unlocks the divine life, the destiny, the health, and the wealth of all those individuals and nations that love it. What is revelation? It is none other than the fruit of divine inspiration. All who turn to God and draw from Him, will be shown the things they need to know at that moment. This is revelation.

As you seek God daily, He will show you many things, not all at once, but step by step, or, as Isaiah says, *"Precept upon precept, line upon line" (Isaiah 28:10)*. Revelation has a progressive aspect, with each new insight building on what went before. Amongst the many things you will learn from Heaven, will be a developing understanding of your God-given role, your mission, your purpose in life.

You will probably find that this includes both a general sense of your calling, as well as specific daily guidance. Firstly, God will give you a sense of your overall mission, and of the nature of the part you have been called to play on the stage of life. Whether more or less detailed at the start, this understanding will develop and deepen as you walk with Him. Secondly, He will give you specific directions as you need them, on how to fulfil your mission. Each morning, if you will listen, Heaven will give you your orders for the day, those things you must do to fulfil the will of God.

These daily directions will rarely be complicated, but will usually be steps easy to understand. Of course, they may or may not be what we expect to hear. It is imperative that we come to God in full submission to His will. Our plans, however well informed by human wisdom, must bow to His. We may not always see the wisdom of God's directions at the time we receive them, but we certainly will in time, for wisdom is always justified by her children.

Having received your daily directions from Heaven, see to the matter that day. This is the way of the heavenly man or woman. Boaz, an ancestor of Jesus Christ, was such a man. When God called him to act on behalf of Ruth, a close relation of his, he attended to it the very same day.

Knowing that he was such a man, Naomi, Ruth's mother-in-law, reassured her with the words:

> *Sit still, my daughter, until you know how the matter will turn out; for the man will not rest until he has concluded the matter this day.*   Ruth 3:18

Unless it is clear that the directions refer to a later date or event, we should make doing them a priority for the day we are in. Nothing is more important than doing the will of Heaven.

The words of Mary, the mother of Jesus, to the stewards at the wedding in Cana of Galilee, are as relevant to us today as they were to their first century recipients. The wine had run out and the organisers did not know what to do. So they approached Mary for advice, and she pointed them to Jesus. Her directions could not have been clearer:

> *Whatever He says to you, do it.*   John 2:5

Mary's words ring out across the centuries, challenging all who hear to, *"Be doers of the word, and not hearers only" (James 1:22)*. Whatever your need, if you will turn to Jesus, and do what He says, He will make a way, even where there is no way. When the wedding stewards at Cana did what Jesus told them to do, a miracle took place. Water was turned to wine, and not just any wine, but wine of the finest quality. As you learn to accurately discern the Master's voice, and you do what He tells you to do, you will discover that, given time, things not only work out, but that they work out in the best way. Whether results appear in moments, or take many years to come to fruition, the fruit of obedience to divine inspiration will be to that of idolatrous self-dependence what fine wine is to water.

XV
WHEN IT'S HARD TO HEAR

What about those times when you seek God and hear nothing? There are times when this is the experience of everyone who listens to God, and there are a variety of reasons for it.

INATTENTION

The most common cause is probably a lack of attention or concentration. We listen, but we are not listening properly. As a result, we either hear nothing, or we hear one of the other voices in the human mind, such as the voice of our hopes, or that of our fears. If we continue to be careless in the way that we listen, we may confuse such voices with God's and make many unnecessary and avoidable mistakes. This problem can easily be corrected by paying proper attention. When we actively focus our inner attention on the Lord, and test what we receive with our spirit, we are much less likely to make such mistakes. If you hear nothing, check your focus, make any adjustments that are necessary, and carry on.

TIREDNESS

A related cause is that of tiredness. With growing exhaustion and fatigue, it may become increasingly hard to concentrate in this way, making it difficult to hear. Often the best thing in such cases is simply to trust God and rest. After a night's sleep you will likely find it easier to focus your mind. On those occasions where you feel that you must have an answer, you may decide to push on. Sometimes a strong coffee, or some brisk exercise, may give your body the jolt it needs in order to concentrate. If, despite your persistence, you find that you are unable to break through (I have sometimes found myself falling asleep when I desperately needed to hear from Heaven), don't beat yourself up, but take the rest that you need. God is not limited by your human frailty and will make a way. When you've slept a bit, get back to prayer.

A CLOSED MIND

Sometimes we do not hear because our minds are closed. Perhaps we are only prepared to hear God say certain things, such as words that agree with our own point of view. If we are not fully open to God, we will be unable to fully hear Him. We should subjugate our own thoughts to the mind of Christ within us. As we yield our minds to Him, He will lift them to new and greater heights of insight and understanding. This is a dramatic expansion of the mind and its capabilities, not a diminution. The aim is not that you cease to have your own opinions, views, or convictions. God has no use for mindless followers, empty-headed persons, robotic humans who seek to be controlled. But He does seek those who will submit their views, however strongly held, to Him. He desires a yielded mind, not an empty one.

GOD IS SILENT

Another possible reason for our failing to hear is that God is silent. It might be unwise to assume that God is talking incessantly to each one of us. During His life on earth, there were times when Christ was silent, moments made the more dramatic, and messages made the more eloquent, by His lack of words. If this was the case with Christ's earthly communications, why should it not be so with messages from Heaven? In the book of Revelation, John observes that Heaven itself was silent for the space of half an hour.

There are times when we must wait for God, times when we listen, but there is no immediate reply. At such times, we watch and we wait. As Habakkuk said, *"I will stand my watch and set myself on the rampart, and watch to see what He will say to me" (Habakkuk 2:1).* Though the vision tarries, like Habakkuk we wait for it, *"Because it will surely come" (Habakkuk 2:3).* If when you listen, God is silent, persevere — the word will come. And if silence is the message, heed it.

Spiritual Warfare

Intense spiritual warfare represents another situation in which it may be hard to hear God. Given that earth is locked in a battle between spiritual forces of good and evil, it is impossible for any human life to remain unaffected. Thankfully, Heaven's final victory is guaranteed, for the forces in this conflict are unevenly matched, the power of the Almighty being infinitely greater than that of Satan. But until that time, the war continues unabated, and those who would seek God must be ready to resist the devil in his attempts to stop them. *"Submit to God,"* says James. *"Resist the devil and he will flee from you"* (James 4:7). Take your stand of resistance, and maintain it for as long as necessary.

Probably the most common form of spiritual attack is the demonic bombardment of the mind with wrong, unhelpful, fearful, or negative thoughts. Such thoughts are not always the result of demonic influence, but when they are their foul sources must be vigorously opposed. Whenever you find yourself the victim of such an onslaught, do not indulge or entertain any ideas of this nature. Do not feed on these ideas, for they are poisonous to your soul. Instantly command Satan and his demons to leave you, in

Jesus name, and turn your mind to God. Listen to Him — feed both on His personal word to you, and on His written word, the Bible. Listening may not be as easy as at other times, but it is perfectly possible. By resisting in this way, you will strengthen yourself, and defeat your infernal opponent, who *will* depart from you. Until he does, stay calm, trusting in God, and standing on the truth of His word.

Spiritual warfare can take other forms, such as a demonically inspired oppression or heaviness that can weigh upon a person, making it difficult, or even impossible, for them to engage in their usual work, or other activities. The answer to this is the same as for the ideational bombardment of the mind — seek the Lord!

Stop what you are doing, if possible, and get down to prayer. Look to Heaven, listen to God, and continue listening for as long as it takes. In time, the attack will pass. Sometimes it will pass quickly. At other times it may take longer, and on occasions significantly longer. In some circumstances you may need to pray for an extended period of hours, or even days, before the spiritual battle is won.

During such times of darkness, you may not be able to work, for there is a night in which no one can continue their labour. As Jesus said:

I must work the works of Him who sent Me while it is day; the night is coming when no one can work.

John 9:4

Even where the darkness is so deep that you can no longer work, or maintain your usual life and activities, you must continue to stand firm in your faith. In the words of Saint Paul:

Finally, my brethren, be strong in the Lord and in the power of His might. Put on the whole armour of God that you may be able to stand against the wiles of the devil, for we do not wrestle against flesh and blood, but against principalities, against powers, against the rulers of the darkness of this age, against spiritual hosts of wickedness in the heavenly places. Therefore take up the whole armour of God that you may be able to withstand in the evil day, and having done all, to stand. Stand therefore, having girded your waist with truth, having put on the breastplate of righteousness, and having shod your feet with the preparation of the gospel of peace; above all, taking the shield of faith with which you will be able to quench all the fiery darts of the wicked one. And take the helmet of salvation, and the sword of the Spirit, which is the word of God; praying always with all prayer and supplication in the Spirit, being watchful to this end with all perseverance and supplication for all the saints. Ephesians 6:10-18

Stand your ground, looking and listening to Heaven. Learn to seek God in the storms of life, whether those storms are of natural, human, or demonic origin, and you will do well. I recall what God said to me on one occasion when I was facing spiritual opposition: *"Simon, you are going through a storm. Stand firm. There's never been a storm that didn't pass. All you must do is stand. You will still be standing when the storm ends, ready to resume your work!"*

DISAPPOINTMENT, DEPRESSION & DESPAIR

Before we leave this subject, mention should be made of the difficulties encountered in seeking God by those who are feeling down or depressed. Many spiritual men and women over the centuries, including a good number of biblical heroes, appear to have battled with the darkness of disappointment, depression, and despair. Spiritual symptoms of depression can include a sense of God's remoteness or absence, as well as uncharacteristic doubts in relation to matters of faith. Combine these with cognitive symptoms, such as a tendency to negative thinking and poor concentration, and you can see how depression may threaten a person's experience of the spiritual life.

Depression may be a complex problem with various causes. Whilst a proper description of its diagnosis and treatment lies outside the scope of this book, it is appropriate to say something about the management of depression in relation to the Way of Heaven. Though the depressed person may feel remote from God, or even separated from Him, there is no reason why they should not continue to daily seek God, and every reason why they should, for such meditation is the greatest spiritual medicine in the treatment of depression.

The experience of God is the most potent force in mastering and defeating disappointment, depression, and despair. When you are down, whether that is simply feeling a little sad, or experiencing major depression, seek God.

Whatever dark thoughts and painful feelings assail you, whatever your state of mental or physical health, hold fast to God and don't let go. Stand on the Rock, and on the Rock you will remain. Short or long, the storm will pass, and there will be calm.

In each succeeding storm of whatever kind (you must pass through many if you would win the prize), practise this, and you will grow stronger and stronger in faith, until your heart is fully established. Finally, like Christ, you will sleep through the storm.

XVI
UNBROKEN COMMUNION

How much of Heaven do you want? It's up to you. You can have as much, or as little, as you desire.

Like all disciplines, learning to seek God is a process that takes time to be mastered, but once learnt, this discipline may be exercised as often as we wish. We may become those who only seek God occasionally, or we may press towards the goal of becoming a competent ambassador of Heaven, one who consistently receives and faithfully follows the guidance of the Eternal.

Some will never attain this level of spiritual prosperity, not because they lack the ability, but because they lack the willingness to fully trust Heaven's King. As Christ makes clear:

> *No one can serve two masters; for either he will hate the one and love the other, or else he will be loyal to the one and despise the other.*   Matthew 6:24

The Way of Heaven is for the single-minded, those who have set their face to seek and serve One Lord. The double-minded person cannot fully take this Way, for they are unable to commit wholly to Heaven's cause.

As James points out:

> He who doubts is like a wave of the sea driven and tossed by the wind ... he is a double-minded man, unstable in all his ways.   *James 1:6,8*

We have been offered nothing less than unbroken communion with God. The way to Heaven is open. Will we be occasional visitors who come to God only when we face difficulties, or will we make it our goal to walk with Him? Any time spent looking and listening to Heaven, however short, is good, but to dwell here is better by far. The writer of Hebrews talks of:

> Looking unto Jesus, the author and finisher of our faith, who for the joy that was set before Him endured the cross, despising the shame, and has sat down at the right hand of the throne of God.   *Hebrews 12:2*

The life of faith is lived most fully in unceasing fellowship with God. It is a daily walk with Jesus.

This does not mean that we must all become hermits, withdrawing from the world in order to devote our lives solely to prayer. This may be the calling of some, but it is not what we are talking about here. Unbroken communion is attainable by all, and may be enjoyed in any setting, however busy, stressful, or demanding.

Neither does it mean that we will consciously hear God every moment of the day. Communion is a quality of relationship, a oneness born of love. It includes both listening and hearing, but it is far more than both of these, for they are simply two expressions of loving relationship. To commune with God is to enjoy His company at all times and in all places.

Love is the key that unlocks the Way of Heaven. If God is your first love, you will turn to Him often, you will be concerned to know His will, you will aim to please Him in all things, and when you sin you will be sorry, turning from sin in your heart.

It was love that made it possible for us to take this Way:

For God so loved the world that He gave His only begotten Son, that whoever believes in Him should not perish but have everlasting life. John 3:16

Come to God and you will experience love, for love is His nature. If you seek God, you will find Him, and if you find Him, you will love Him. David says: *"Oh, taste and see that the Lord is good" (Psalm 34:8).* Love is the fruit of an encounter with God, and those who walk with Him will walk in love.

If you have tasted of the goodness of God, if you have experienced His love, then abide here by faith, for on believing that you are loved, all your strength is founded.

As John says, this is a perfect love that drives out fear, a love that emboldens, establishes, and empowers:

And we have known and believed the love that God has for us. God is love, and he who abides in love abides in God, and God in him. Love has been perfected among us in this: that we may have boldness in the day of judgement; because as He is, so are we in this world. There is no fear in love; but perfect love casts out fear, because fear involves torment. But he who fears has not been made perfect in love. We love Him because He first loved us.   I John 4:16-19

The Way of Heaven is the way of love, from start to finish. The Son of God went to the cross for love's sake, for where there is love, there is sacrifice. When we come to Him He enfolds us in His love, that we might rest there and from this place of eternal security, love as we are loved.

Make God your first love, and you will die to your old self and live to Him, discovering your new regenerate nature and your heavenly mission on earth. It is in this place of loving communion that your faith will be fully effective:

For in Christ Jesus neither circumcision nor uncircumcision avails anything, but faith working by love.   Galatians 5:6

Live in love, and you will do love's work, for as Jesus said:

If you love Me, you will keep My commandments.
John 14:15

If we love God, we will look to Him often, and as a result, develop a growing awareness of His presence with us. There are times when this will be a more conscious focus, but at other times, such as when we are concentrating on a particular task, it will be more a matter of knowing that what we do, we do in His presence.

Your conscious communion with God will grow as you exercise it. Not only will you find it easier to focus your attention on Him, but you will also find that you are increasingly able to look to Him whilst doing other things. This is largely due to the remarkable capacity of humans to do two or more things at the same time. Carefully analyse most of the complex tasks that people perform, and you will find them made up of various component skills. Walking across a room, driving a car, and playing a musical instrument, are all examples of activities in which people do a number of things simultaneously. There is absolutely no reason why, with practice, one should not be able to extend one's awareness of God so that one is enjoying His presence with ever increasing continuity.

Sadly, there are some who never seek God. Others look to Him for a short time each day, and leave it at that. Then there are those who turn to Him at various points during the day, or when faced with problems and challenges on which they seek His illumination and guidance. Finally, there are those who practice the presence of God as often as they can. You are called to walk with Him. Don't settle for less.

Follow your love for God. Indulge it, and let it fill your life. Picture the Lord with you, in every aspect of your day. In everything you do, imagine that you are doing it with Jesus. See Him there, by your side, as you walk, as you talk, as you eat, as you work. And whenever you are not engaged in a task that requires your total concentration, focus your attention more fully on Him. Even when you are involved in necessarily focused activity, you will find that, because you picture Christ with you in it, He may speak to you from time to time, telling you those things you need to know.

Whenever you become aware that you have forgotten Him, pull your mind back to its true focus, the object of your greatest love. Put Jesus back in the picture. Imagine Him with you. See Him with your inner eye and listen to Him with your inner ear. What do you see? What does He say?

As in the learning of any set of skills, you will need to practice this repeatedly, and to continue practising it consciously and deliberately until it becomes your automatic and unconscious behaviour. Do what you love, and you will grow stronger in it. Love what you do, and it will grow stronger in you. Keep bringing Jesus to mind and keeping

Him there. Practice living in the awareness of His presence. The more you practice, the better you'll get, and the greater your communication with Heaven will be.

Your friend, the all-knowing and all-powerful God, is with you. Why live as though you were on your own? Enjoy unbroken communion with Him and make the most of your life here on earth.

XVII
DIVINE ORGANISATION

Divine inspiration is as vital to the success of groups as it is to that of individuals. When groups of people seek God and obey His commands, whether they are friends, families, colleagues, teams, organisations, nations, or groups of nations, true success and eternal rewards are theirs.

People in groups have different roles, and for these roles to work together effectively there must be organisation. But who's organisation? The structures and cultures of human organisations, whether small and great, come in various shapes and forms. To begin to understand how organisations of every kind may take the Way of Heaven, we must look at leaders.

Who are the leaders in any group of people? The defining quality of leadership is the stimulus to change. Leaders lead. Others are changed by their influence in some way. Whether you hold a formal leadership role or not, whenever anyone changes as a result of your behaviour, you are leading. In other words, we are all potential leaders, though we may not know it.

True leadership is transcendental, that is, it has its source in Heaven. As anyone seeks the will of Heaven and follows it, they fulfil their destiny as a leader, becoming a mighty force for constructive change in the lives of others. If, in addition, they hold a formal leadership position within a group, that influence may be greatly magnified, as the group itself takes the Way of Heaven. However, much may depend on the spirituality of individual group members. As more of them take the Way of Heaven, so the total positive impact of the whole group is optimised.

Joshua, in his leadership of ancient Israel, demonstrates his clear understanding of this vital principle when he invites his people to make a fundamental choice. He says:

> *Choose for yourselves this day whom you will serve, whether the gods which your fathers served that were on the other side of the River, or the gods of the Amorites, in whose land you dwell.*   Joshua 24:15a

And then, having asked them to choose, he leads them by example with the assertion, *"But as for me and my house, we will serve the Lord" (Joshua 24:15b)*. Rather than give a directive to serve God, Joshua wisely gives his people the freedom to choose for themselves.

Had he ordered them to seek and serve God, he might have gained their compliance, but he would not have won their hearts. He knew that forced allegiance could never yield true success, so he took a risk, a risk many leaders are unwilling to take. He recognised and affirmed the right of his people to make their own choice.

The choice before the people that day was of the most fundamental significance, for it was a choice between sources of inspiration. Would they choose the Way of

Heaven, or would they worship other gods? Joshua knew that if the people rejected God, they would be divided and fall but if they chose to serve the Lord, there would be unity and success.

When each member of a group looks to God, learns how to hear accurately, and does what He says, there is greater agreement, each working together with the others in a more harmonious way. To the extent that they are divinely inspired, individuals are divinely organised together in the fulfilment of God's plans and the achievement of His purposes. The divinely inspired organisation is the perfect organisational form. Joshua understood that, which is why he asked his people to choose where they would look for inspiration and guidance. He hoped they would choose Heaven, and he knew that if they did, his job as leader would be a whole lot easier, for the guidance they would receive from Heaven would be congruent with his own. Joshua wanted his people with him, and he knew that the best way to achieve this was to let them choose for themselves in the matter of divine inspiration. If, like him, they chose to follow God, they would all move forwards together as one.

Joshua's predecessor Moses was also keenly aware of this truth. An inspirational leader of the first order, Moses always respected the individual's right to choose. Despite seeing his people use their choice to reject God on several occasions, even making themselves idols to worship, Moses never changed his position, but continued in the divinely inspired conviction that the greatest people were those who all freely chose to serve the Lord together. This view is clearly behind his response to being told that some of the people were prophesying. He was delighted and said:

> *Oh, that all the Lord's people were prophets and that the Lord would put His Spirit upon them!*
>
> *Numbers 11:29*

The ideal for Moses was a divinely inspired organisation. He longed that everyone would love and serve God as he did.

To encourage choice as a leader is to risk division and loss of support, which is why some deny the right of choice to others, substituting government by human authority for organisation under divine inspiration. Like God, wise leaders choose the latter path. This was the Way of Heaven from the beginning. The first people, created by God and placed in an idyllic environment, were entirely free to choose whether or not they would follow Him. We know from Genesis that, tempted by the devil's lie that they would be better off by following his ideas, they chose to reject God's guidance. The result of choosing to follow Satan was, as we know, catastrophic.

In that moment, humanity was separated from God by sin, but He had already prepared a way back, and a Rescuer, *"Foreordained before the foundation of the world" (I Peter 1:20)*. The separation could only end with removal of the sin that stood in the way. So God did just that. He came to earth as a man, and took the sin of all upon Himself that the way might be cleared. As John says:

> For God so loved the world that He gave His only begotten Son, that whoever believes in Him should not perish but have everlasting life.   John 3:16

Compassionate rulers, like the King of Heaven, guide rather than coerce. They show the Way, but they do not force it upon their people. They understand that the people must choose for themselves and they affirm that right, being prepared to work with the people, whatever they may choose. If they choose the good, the group may advance quickly in the will of Heaven, but if they choose to reject the Way of Heaven, the leaders must work hard to bring them back into the Way. The leader who walks with God, and teaches the people to walk with God, is truly great.

Sadly, it is often the case that leaders prefer to follow their own counsel, rather than seek the counsel of Heaven. I was once asked by the leaders of an organisation to give my opinion on what I thought God was saying to them as an organisation. Knowing them to be believers, I was a little surprised by this request. "Have they not sought God themselves?" I wondered. We were sitting together in the office of the senior director, and it was clear that they wanted an answer there and then. Quickly I prayed within myself, looking to the Lord for His answer. In a moment it came to me, in the form of three visions. In the first vision I saw a mountain, or to be more precise, a somewhat stylised picture of a mountain. As I looked, I realised that this was the symbol of the Paramount film company. "What does this mean?" I thought to myself. Then the second vision appeared: a moving picture of a strong lion who roared mightily. I recognised it immediately as the symbol of the MGM film company. Finally, the third vision came to me. It was a muscular man striking a gong, the symbol of the J Arthur Rank film company. At first I did not understand the meaning or the message of these visions. "How unusual," I thought, "for God to give me such pictures." Unable to see the meaning for myself, I asked God to reveal it to me, which He instantly did. All this happened in a brief moment of time, so that, hardly had they made their request, I was ready to answer. "God has given me three pictures," I said, before proceeding to describe each in turn. "The message is this: the success of any film depends upon the actors and actresses following the guidance of the Director. If they reject the Director and refuse to follow the script, choosing instead to do what each wants, the result will be chaotic rather than organised, confused rather than clear, worthless rather than valuable. So it is with those who will not look to God, nor follow His directions. They will neither be organised according to Heaven's will, nor will they achieve all that God has planned for them. The conclusion is clear: seek God, all of you, and do His will. Make it your first priority as leaders to learn to seek God daily, and encourage every member of your organisation to do the same. Do this and you will fulfil your divine destiny." Sadly, my words appeared to fall on deaf ears. These leaders seemed unwilling to fully submit their leadership to God's. The result was what it always is when the Director is not followed: the loss of the good that would have been.

I have always been convinced that the message I received that day is God's message to all groups and their members. For those who receive it, whether families or nations, this message of heavenly organisation will transform their life together and make them great in the eyes of Heaven. Let God direct your family, your team, your business, your board, and your nation. The results will prove the wisdom of your choice.

XVIII
FRIENDS IN HEAVEN'S CAUSE

There came a point in the relationship between Christ and His disciples when their life together changed forever. It was not a sudden transformation, but the conclusion of a gradual process that had begun when they first met. They had followed Him from the beginning, watching, listening, questioning, learning, and making mistakes. They had seen ancient prophecy fulfilled, the sick healed, the dead raised, miracles, signs and wonders. They had felt the opposition of His enemies and the enormity of His mission. They had been tested again and again, and had now reached a place where Jesus could say to them:

> *You are My friends if you do whatever I command you. No longer do I call you servants, for the servant does not know what his master does. But I have called you friends, for all things that I have heard from My Father, I have made know to you.   John 15:14&15*

It is clear from Christ's words that friendship with God is contingent upon obedience to Him. We are His friends if we do whatever He commands us.

If you are not already a friend of God, let me tell you now that He wants you as a friend, but not merely a friend. Friendship is a relational quality, but its presence says nothing about the level of contact. For example, I may have a good friend who I only meet or talk with on rare occasions. From my experience, it seems to me that this is the kind of relationship that some people want to have with God. They want to know that God is their friend, and to enjoy the sense of inner security that this conviction brings, both in relation to their temporal life, and the life of the world to come, but they don't want to do what God says, preferring to do things in their own way. Many of them like to believe that they are doing what God wants them to do, but the sad truth is that they have not received their orders from Heaven. Rather, their plans and purposes are of their own creation, informed perhaps by scriptural wisdom and principles, but still their own will, not God's. Some may chose this position out of ignorance, not realising that God speaks today, and that daily communication with Him is normative. Others choose it because they will not submit to His lordship. They may love God deeply, and they may strongly desire to do His will, but they will not yield wholly to Him, preferring to keep full executive control of their lives. By so doing, such people refuse God His rightful place in their hearts, relegating Him to subservience or even irrelevance. Instead of God occupying the throne of their heart, they occupy it themselves, and mess things up!

God not only seeks your friendship. He wants to work with you. There's a job to be done, a work of eternal significance that requires your full and informed commitment. That work is the redemption of humanity.

God's purpose has always been that people might enjoy the highest quality of life that Heaven affords. He created a perfect environment for the first humans, but sadly it was lost when they turned from Him to follow Satan's wicked proposal. God was determined to restore that which had been lost, and for this purpose gave His Son to die in our place, carrying the sin of all in His body on the cross. Christ declared Heaven's manifesto on earth, contrasting it with Satan's evil purpose:

> *The thief comes to steal, to kill, and to destroy," He said, "But I have come that you might have life, and have it more abundantly.* John 10:10

Through His atoning death, resurrection, and ascension into Heaven, Christ fulfilled His divine mission, opening up a way back for anyone who wanted it, a way back to God, and to the life that only God can give. We are called to play our part in this, the greatest of all projects, working together with God, as He seeks to draw all men and women into personal relationship with Himself.

This work cannot be properly done apart from God, for only He sees and knows all. Working with Him, under His daily guidance and direction, we will do and say those things that promote the true well being of everyone with whom we come into contact. God invites us, not only to become His friends, but also His fellow labourers, those who hear from Heaven and obey.

You and I may never meet, but we may be friends in the Way, those whose first commitment is to love and serve the Lord. As friends in Heaven's cause, we are united in one mission: to fulfil the will of God on earth. This we do by looking to Jesus, the author and finisher of our faith.

We start each day with praise and thanksgiving to God, turning to Him in order to receive whatever He would communicate to us, including our directions for the day.

We endeavour to spend each day in the awareness of His presence, regularly turning to Him for His thoughts and guidance on each matter.

We end each day in celebration of His love, reviewing with Him our fulfilment of His directions for the day, and praying as we fall asleep, the unconscious prayer of our heart rising to Heaven until the morning comes.

BY THE SAME AUTHOR

TODAY

DAILY MEDITATIONS FOR ABUNDANT LIVING

ISBN 978-0-9562559-0-7

MAXIMISED MINDPOWER

MAKING THE MOST OF YOUR MIND

ISBN 978-0-9562559-5-2

Available from Inspirational Faith at
todayonline.biz

Lightning Source UK Ltd.
Milton Keynes UK

174470UK00003B/6/P